Out of This World

The Amazing Search for an Alien Earth

Jacob Berkowitz

Kids Can Press

In memory of Mr. Gerry Elmes, my grade six teacher. He encouraged us to tell our stories. — J.B.

Acknowledgments

This book is possible thanks to the curiosity, perseverance and hard work of thousands of astronomers and astrobiologists. These scientists, engineers and technicians really are stellar. Many of them work for NASA or the European Space Agency. A special thanks to: Dr. David Charbonneau, Thomas D. Cabot Associate Professor of Astronomy, Harvard-Smithsonian Center for Astrophysics, Harvard University; Dr. Dan Werthimer, Director of SETI program, University of California, Berkeley; Dr. Robert Hurt, Spitzer Science Center at the California Institute of Technology, Pasadena, California; Dr. Sara Seager, Ellen Swallow Richards Associate Professor of Planetary Science, Massachusetts Institute of Technology; Dr. James Hesser, National Research Council Canada, Director, Dominion Astrophysical Observatory, Hertzberg Institute of Astrophysics; Dr. Ian A. Crawford, School of Earth Sciences, Birkbeck College, London, England; Olathe MacIntyre, MSc, PhD candidate in the Controlled Environment Systems Research Facility, Department of Environmental Biology, University of Guelph; Eric Chisholm, National Research Council Canada, Manager, Centre of the Universe interpretive center, Hertzberg Institute for Astrophysics, Canada; and Dr. Stephen Maran, the former press officer for the American Astronomical Society, who kept my e-mail in-box filled with interesting exoplanet news.

The writing of this book benefited from the financial support of the Ontario Arts Council via Ontario taxpayers, and I'm grateful for the support of the Robert Bosch Foundation (Germany) for introducing me to the wonder of exoplanets.

A big shout-out to my editor, Valerie Wyatt, who only made the story better, and to Céleste Gagnon for the great Ambrosia drawings. Thanks to all the staff at KCP for the care and effort they put into launching this book.

Kids Can Press acknowledges the financial support of the Government of Ontario, through the Ontario Media Development Corporation's Ontario Book Initiative, and the Government of Canada, through the BPIDP, for our publishing activity.

Published in Canada by
Kids Can Press Ltd.
29 Birch Avenue
Toronto, ON M4V 1E2

Published in the U.S. by
Kids Can Press Ltd.
2250 Military Road
Tonawanda, NY 14150

www.kidscanpress.com

Edited by Valerie Wyatt
Designed by Marie Bartholomew
Illustrations by Céleste Gagnon

Printed and bound in Singapore

The hardcover edition of this book is smyth sewn casebound.

The paperback edition of this book is limp sewn with a drawn-on cover.

CM 09   0 9 8 7 6 5 4 3 2 1
CM PA 09 0 9 8 7 6 5 4 3 2 1

Library and Archives Canada Cataloguing in Publication

Berkowitz, Jacob
    Out of this world : the amazing search for an alien earth /
Jacob Berkowitz.

ISBN 978-1-55453-197-4 (bound).
ISBN 978-1-55453-198-1 (pbk.)

1. Life on other planets—Juvenile literature. 2. Outer space—Exploration—Juvenile literature. I. Title.

QB54.B375 2009   j576.8'39   C2008-908109-9

Kids Can Press is a *Corus*™ Entertainment company

Contents

One Night on Xenon

It is a beautiful clear night on Xenon. Everywhere on the dark side of the planet, families are looking up at the magic of the night sky.

"Wow! There are so many stars," says Ambrosia.

Ambrosia is a Xenon clone. Tonight she's with her modad — her one parent. She loves coming to Xenon's surface, where the air is thick with sulfur. It smells like rotten eggs. Delicious!

Xenon is locked in an ice age that has lasted 10 000 years. Almost everyone lives below ground. Ambrosia has seen pictures of Xenon before the ice covered it. Her favorite is the one of the blue sunset and the red sky. And she's read about rain. Imagine — liquid water falling from the sky! Tonight, though, she's looking at the stars.

"Do you think there are people on other planets?" she asks.

Modad pulls her close. "Probably. The universe is enormous. There could be lots of aliens."

A siren sounds. It's time for everyone to go underground for the night. Ambrosia looks through her telescope one last time, peering at the faintest stars. She makes a silent promise: *When I grow up, I'm going out there to explore!*

Ambrosia looks at a beautiful cluster of stars. The blue ones are hot, newly formed young stars.

The Amazing Search for Alien Earth

When you look up at the night sky, do you wonder if there are aliens on distant planets? Or are we alone in the universe? You're definitely not the only one asking these questions. For thousands of years Earthlings have been wondering whether there is life anywhere else in the universe.

But now something is different. For the first time in human history, we don't have to just dream about aliens — we can actually search for them.

Astrobiologists are scientists who are exploring for alien life. No, they aren't looking for UFOs (Unidentified Flying Objects) or signs of alien visits to Earth. They're looking for something much bigger — an Alien Earth.

What is an Alien Earth? Not another planet exactly like ours, but one that, like Earth, is alive. It's a planet where the atmosphere, water, rocks, animals and plants are all part of one big system we call *life*. For example, imagine Earth without an atmosphere. *Gasp!* We wouldn't be able to breathe, plus we'd be roasted by the sun's ultraviolet radiation. And without plants, Earth's atmosphere would be very different — there wouldn't be any breathable oxygen in it. Astrobiologists think the best way to find aliens is to look for a planet they'd call home, an Alien Earth.

As you read this, astrobiologists are using high-tech space gear to look and listen for an Alien Earth. Robotic spacecraft sent from Earth are searching for life on moons and other planets in our solar system. And we're using telescopes, including ones in space high above the Earth, to look for living planets around other stars in the Milky Way galaxy.

The best part of all? It's possible that an Alien Earth will be discovered during *your* lifetime. Yes, it's countdown time in the search for Alien Earth, and you've got a window seat!

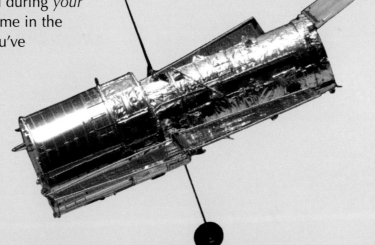

The Hubble Space Telescope is helping in the search for an Alien Earth.

UFO or NO?

Have aliens already found us? Every year thousands of people report seeing UFOs. Some even claim they've been *aboard* alien spaceships. The most famous UFO story is of a flying saucer that reportedly crashed near Roswell, New Mexico, in 1947. There's even a UFO Museum in Roswell.

But there is no scientific evidence that Earth has ever been visited by aliens. No alien bodies, footprints or spaceship parts — just people's stories. It's up to astrobiologists to turn alien fantasy into fact.

This is what our home galaxy, the Milky Way, would look like seen from another galaxy. Is Earth the only living planet among the 300 billion stars of the Milky Way? Only time will tell.

This is a fake UFO picture. To make one yourself, turn to page 39.

Aliens on Earth?

Where do you start a search for an Alien Earth? Not with a telescope but with a microscope. Astrobiologists begin their alien search by looking for tiny, far-out life right here at home.

Why? Other planets are much colder or hotter than most places on Earth. To help figure out if these planets could be alive, astrobiologists search for life in the most extreme environments on Earth. They look in the boiling hot water around undersea volcanoes and drill down under glaciers to ask, "Is anybody home?" The answer is almost always "Yes!"

Scientists call the creatures that live in Earth's most extreme places extremophiles. The "philos" in "extremophile" is the Greek word for love. These creatures don't just like harsh conditions — they love them!

Extremophiles are making astrobiologists think twice about the types of planets that could be alive. Other planets might have conditions that would freeze or fry us humans, but extremophiles are proof that an extreme Alien Earth could be home sweet home for some life forms.

Tartigrades, commonly called water bears, are some of Earth's toughest creatures. These microscopic animals survived a trip into outer space — without spacesuits!

Extremophile Olympians

Most extremophiles are microscopic creatures such as bacteria. Although they are small, these tiny Earthlings are big at pushing life right to the very limits.

Acid Champ: *Ferroplasma acidarmanus*

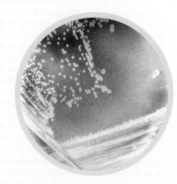

Don't even think about tracking down this extreme champion to offer congratulations. It thrives in the one of the most acidic places on Earth: wastewater from metal mines. The waste water is 10 000 times more acidic than vinegar and would dissolve you into a pile of mush.

Radiation Champ: *Deinococcus radiodurans*

You'd die if you hung out with this radiation record-holder. This super-bacterium can survive 1000 times more radiation than any other creature on Earth. It can even live inside nuclear power reactors.

Heat Champ: *Pyrolobus fumarii*

For this extraordinary extremophile, a hot tub would be a cold bath. It lives on the walls of black smokers, which are volcano-shaped spouts that eject boiling-hot water from the ocean floor. This bacterium won't even grow if the thermostat dips below a scorching 90°C (194°F).

A mechanical arm on the Alvin submersible reaches out for a sample from a black smoker hydrothermal vent deep under the Pacific Ocean.

Life in the Deep Freeze

In the Arctic and Antarctic, many extremophiles can survive for thousands of years in permafrost (frozen soil). To see what happens when average-o-philes (like us) hit the deep freeze, try this experiment.

Put a piece of fresh lettuce in a container and put the container in the freezer. Leave it there for a day. Remove the frozen lettuce and let it thaw to room temperature. What happened to it?

The cells in the lettuce are full of water. When this water freezes into ice it expands, and the sharp ice crystals break the cells. The result is mushy lettuce. Extremophiles that live in freezing temperatures have antifreeze in their cells. The antifreeze prevents the formation of deadly ice.

Fresh   Frozen and thawed

Mars: Is Alien Earth Next Door?

For a long time people believed an Alien Earth was right next door. More than 100 years ago, Italian astronomer Giovanni Schiaparelli observed Mars through a telescope and saw what looked like huge canals on the planet's surface. Who could have built canals? Some astronomers thought there must be Martians.

In 1976 we got our first close-up look at Mars. NASA's *Viking I* and *II* robotic spacecraft landed on the red planet to search for life. The planet it revealed was very different from the one people had imagined. Not only were there no canals, Mars looked like a frozen desert with no signs of life. The red planet seemed like a dead planet.

But astrobiologists haven't given up on checking Mars for vital signs of life. They think there are two tantalizing clues that Mars was once alive and might still be today under its red surface.

This photo of Mars, taken by a NASA rover, shows the real surface of Mars. No canals!

Clue No. 1: Water Search

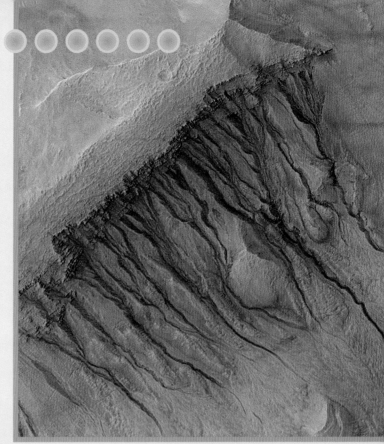

If you're looking for life, astrobiologists say follow the water. That's because on Earth, where there's liquid water, there's life.

On Mars the good news is there's lots of water. The bad news is that it's frozen, mostly at the poles. But the presence of rocks formed in water and dry riverbeds on Mars show that the planet was once warmer and wetter. There were rivers and lakes — maybe with Martians swimming in them. Astrobiologists wonder if there might still be liquid water — and life — hidden under the harsh Martian surface.

Some scientists think that the gullies in the picture on the right were made by flowing water on Mars.

Are the objects in this meteorite evidence of Martian life?

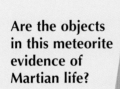

Clue No. 2: Martian in a Meteorite?

What's better than going to Mars to look for life? Having Martians visit you. That's what scientists thought when they cut open this 4.4 billion-year-old, potato-sized chunk of rock found in Antarctica in 1984. It's Martian meteorite ALH84001 — a piece of Mars that was smashed off and sent hurtling through space until it landed on Earth.

The really cool thing is what's inside the meteorite. When scientists sliced it open and zoomed in with a high-powered microscope, they found what looked like a string of pearls. Most amazingly, the "pearls" resembled bacteria found deep below Earth's surface. Could the pearl-like structures be the fossilized remains of ancient *Martian* life? Some astrobiologists think so. Others think the "pearls" are just fancy Martian rock. Without clear evidence, the great astrobiology mystery remains: Is Mars dead — or alive?

School for Alien Explorers

One way to know for sure whether or not Mars is alive is to go there and check for ourselves. Astronauts hope to blast off for the red planet as early as 2031. To get ready to search for life on Mars, astrobiologists are practicing here on Earth by using alien analogue sites — places that resemble Mars but are a lot easier to visit.

You can't get more Mars-like than Devon Island in the Canadian Arctic. It's the site of the Haughton-Mars Project research station. The area is a rocky, polar desert where the thermostat dips to –50ºC (–58°F) in winter — similar to many places near the Martian equator. And when you look out the window, the reddish-brown rocks even *look* like the surface of Mars. It's the perfect place for astrobiologists to test alien search equipment, including robotic vehicles and drilling equipment to check for liquid water and life below the Martian surface.

Astronauts-in-training practice a Martian expedition at the Mars Desert Research Station in Utah, USA.

Mars on Earth

The Mars Desert Research Station in Utah, U.S.A., is another site where astronauts-in-training get alien work experience. To practice for living and working on Mars, six-person crews from around the world spend ten days in "the Hab," short for habitation. It's a big steel can that resembles a possible Martian landing craft.

If you visit the Hab, here are some tips to make you feel like you're really out-of-this-world:

- Set your watch to Martian time. A Martian day is 39 minutes longer than an Earth day.
- Wear your spacesuit outside — always!
- Fix the toilet when it breaks. On Mars an astronaut is also a plumber.

The Hab, short for Habitation, at the Mars Desert Research Station.

Olathe MacIntyre: ET Searcher

What's for dinner on a trip to Mars? Ask Olathe MacIntyre, an astrobiologist with a green thumb. Olathe is a Mars astronaut-in-training whose specialty is growing plants in space. It's a long journey to Mars, and she wants astronauts to get their veggies.

Olathe's space cadet training started at the International Space University in Strasbourg, France. There she studied ways to terraform Mars — to make Mars more Earthlike so that visiting humans would feel more at home. Now Olathe is helping create greenhouses that double as life-support systems. That's because plants grown on spaceships, or on another planet, won't only be for eating. Just as on Earth, the plants' roots will clean water for re-use. The plants will also be oxygen factories, producing oxygen for astronauts to breathe.

Olathe is looking for plants that have the right stuff to grow in space greenhouses. For example, they must be able to survive possible extreme changes in air pressure and solar radiation.

If you're ever a Mars-bound astronaut, you'll have Olathe to thank for making sure that, even in outer space, you'll still have to eat your vegetables.

Venus: Life in the Clouds?

In the race to find another living planet in our solar system, some astrobiologists think the red planet might get nudged out by the yellowish planet: Venus.

In some ways, Venus is Earth's twin — they're about the same size, and both have volcanoes and even lightning. But when it comes to life, Venus has one big problem — the planet is permanently covered with thick clouds of carbon dioxide gas. The clouds trap the sun's heat, pushing the temperature at the surface to more than 400°C (750°F), hot enough to melt some metals. In fact it's so hot that Venus's ancient oceans have boiled away into space.

Was it good-bye water, good-bye any hope of life? Perhaps not. The clouds themselves are like a cool ocean in the sky. *Hmm*, think astrobiologists. *Could there be Venusians living in those clouds?* It's not such a crazy idea. Scientists have recently discovered that Earth's clouds are a great place for bacteria to hang out.

Astrobiologists think the same may be true on Venus. They want to send a robotic spacecraft to scoop up some Venusian cloud and see if there's life in it.

Maat Mons is a volcano on Venus.

An orbiting spacecraft used radar to see through Venus's thick atmosphere and snap this image.

Life Under Icy Moons?

In the search for another living planet, astrobiologists say don't forget to check the moons. Earth's moon appears to be a big, dry rock. But some of the moons of Jupiter and Saturn have icy crusts. Could there be watery life under those frozen shells?

Jupiter's moon Europa is *chil-ly*. Its average surface temperature is about –145°C (–230°F), colder than anywhere on Earth. It's so cold that Europa is covered with a layer of permanent ice 10 km (6 mi.) thick. However, cracks in the ice make astrobiologists think that something is moving under it, possibly an ocean of water up to 100 km (60 mi.) deep.

Saturn's tiny moon Enceladus also has an icy crust. At its south pole are deep cracks that spray out ice crystals in giant geysers 80 km (50 mi.) tall. Some astrobiologists think the icy geysers start out as liquid water.

For both Europa and Enceladus, the big question is, if these moons have liquid water, do they also have life? To know for sure, we'll probably have to send robotic spacecraft on an amazing journey below this alien ice.

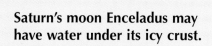

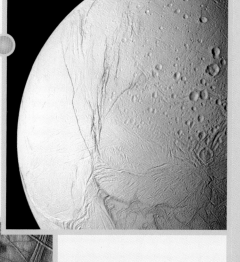

Saturn's moon Enceladus may have water under its icy crust.

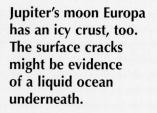

Jupiter's moon Europa has an icy crust, too. The surface cracks might be evidence of a liquid ocean underneath.

Heat from Tides

How can icy moons be warm enough to have liquid water? To see how, try this. Rub your hands together quickly as if warming them up on a cold day. The heat you feel is from friction. Like the ocean tides on Earth, astrobiologists think there are ice tides on the moons of Jupiter and Saturn. The tidal movement of the ice would cause friction — and maybe enough heat to create liquid water.

Discovered : Exoplanets.

In 1995 the search for an Alien Earth got a lot more exciting. Until then we knew for certain of only eight planets in the entire universe, the ones in our solar system. But after years of searching by dozens of astronomers, Michel Mayor and Didier Queloz, working at the Geneva Observatory in Switzerland, discovered an amazing new planet: the first definite exoplanet.

An exoplanet is a planet that's literally out of this solar system. It orbits another star, not our sun. Astronomers have discovered hundreds of exoplanets, and they're sure there are *billions* more to be found. This means there aren't just a couple of other spots in our solar system that alien life might be calling home — the universe is full of them.

An astro-artist's impression of an exoplanet orbiting its star.

The First Exoplanet

No one thought there could be a planet like 51 Pegasus b, the first exoplanet ever discovered. Nicknamed 51 Peg b, this exoplanet is a "hot Jupiter."

It's like Jupiter because it's a giant planet that is mostly made of gas (Jupiter is 318 times more massive than Earth). The main gases in 51 Peg b and Jupiter are hydrogen, the gas that keeps the sun burning, and helium, the lighter-than-air gas used to inflate birthday balloons. But that's where the family resemblance ends. While Jupiter is far from our sun and thus very cold, 51 Peg b is so super-close to its star that it's scorching hot.

Far from being a space oddity, 51 Peg b is pretty normal for an exoplanet. Most of the exoplanets found so far are also hot Jupiters.

Our solar system has a giant gas planet — Jupiter.

Name That Exoplanet

Planets in our solar system are named after characters from Greek and Roman mythology. For example, Jupiter (below) was the ruler of the Greek gods, and Venus was the goddess of love. Exoplanets, however, are mostly named after their star and their order of discovery.

For example, the first exoplanet discovered around the star Upsilon Andromedae is named Upsilon Andromedae *b*, the second planet discovered is Upsilon Andromedae *c*, and the third is Upsilon Andromedae *d*.

Some astrobiologists would like to give, well, friendlier names to exoplanets. Michel Mayor, who co-discovered 51 Peg b, suggested naming it "Epicurus" after the Greek philosopher who 2300 years ago speculated on the possibility of exoplanets.

Tracking Down Exoplanets

One of the most amazing things about exoplanets is that astronomers can find them without actually seeing them. For a long time many astronomers thought it would be impossible to detect planets outside our solar system. That's because an exoplanet orbits in the glare of its star, and the glare is millions of times brighter than the planet itself. So trying to see an exoplanet is like looking into powerful car headlights at night — you're blinded and can't see what's around the light.

Then two Canadian astronomers, Gordon Walker and Bruce Campbell, had a cosmic brain wave: *Maybe we don't need to see the exoplanet.*

Maybe it gives itself away by changing the light we see from its star. Like detectives on a stellar stakeout, they figured out that to spot exoplanets, all you had to do was pay very close attention to their stars. Eureka, they were right!

Most exoplanets are nabbed because their gravity makes their star wobble slightly. Think of holding a dog on a leash. Now imagine the dog running in circles around you. The dog would make you wobble. When a star wobbles, so does the starlight coming from it. So when astronomers see a star whose light is wobbling, they think, *Aha! We've got an exoplanet!*

The twin telescopes at Hawaii's W.M. Keck Observatory help search the Milky Way galaxy for exoplanets.

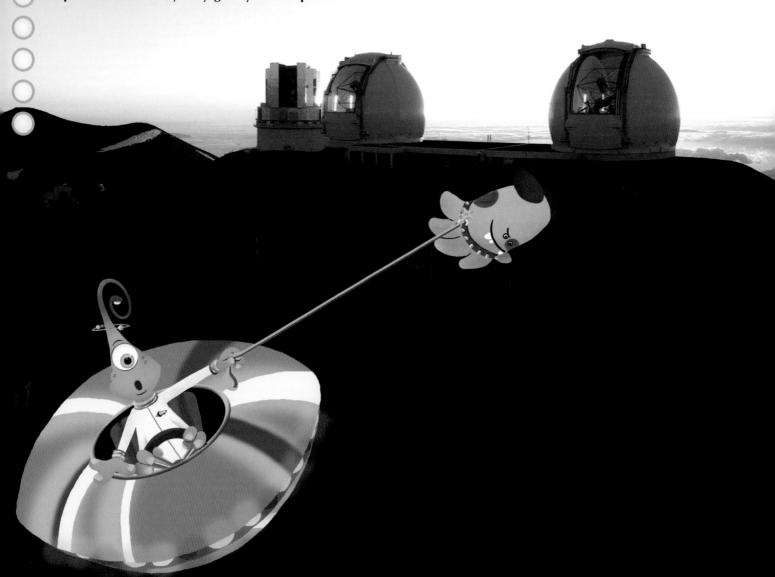

Getting Dimmer

Another way that an exoplanet can get caught is if, during its orbit, it passes in front of its star as viewed from Earth. This "transit" temporarily blocks some of the light astronomers see coming from the star. It's a bit like a moth flying in front of a lamp, causing a tiny drop in the amount of light you'd see. When astronomers see a star get dimmer like this, they know an exoplanet is getting in the way.

An artist's impression of an exoplanet transiting (passing in front of) a distant star.

Astrofact

Most exoplanets found so far are huge, Jupiter-sized ones. These giant exoplanets are much easier to find than smaller, Earth-sized ones.

David Charbonneau: Planet Hunter

David Charbonneau wants to be the first astronomer to find an Alien Earth. And given his stellar track record, he's got the right stuff to pull it off.

When David started university, the first exoplanet had just been found. *Cool,* he thought, *I'd like to find one, too!* The problem was he didn't have a big, expensive telescope. Well, if he couldn't go big, he'd go small. He built a tiny telescope that uses only a telephoto camera lens. But what it lacks in size, it makes up for in patience.

To hunt exoplanets David's telescope, nicknamed Sleuth, stares at a patch of sky for months, taking digital pictures every two minutes. Then a computer program he created scans the images for stars that regularly get dimmer, a telltale sign that an exoplanet is getting in the way.

Using another small telescope called STARE, David helped discover the first exoplanet that transits (passes in front of) its star. Now he's an astronomer at Harvard University, and he has helped find more than six other exoplanets. He's even made the first exoplanet weather report. So discovering an Alien Earth could definitely be in the stars for this ingenious planet hunter.

Postcards from Exoplanets

Astronomers have discovered hundreds of exoplanets so far, and dozens more are spotted every year. There are fiery exoplanets and frozen ones, exoplanets that are super close to their stars and others that are far, far away. The closest exoplanet to Earth is about ten light-years away. A light-year is the distance light travels in a year, about 9461 billion km (5879 billion mi.). It would take one of today's space craft more than 100 000 Earth years to reach it.

Do any of the exoplanets found so far have what it takes to be an Alien Earth? We sent our intrepid space adventurer Ambrosia to check them out and report back.

Dear Earthlings,

Epsilon Eridani b sure is loopy. Earth orbits the sun in an almost perfect circle, which keeps the temperature pretty stable. But this exoplanet takes an egg-shaped trip around its star. It's like being on a hot-and-cold roller coaster — frying when close to the star and freezing when far away. I've had enough of this ride.

Ambrosia

Dear Earthlings,

Whew, it's hot here! OGLE-TR-56b is so near its star that it's roasting. Today the thermometer hit 1704°C (3100°F). It's hot enough that when it rains, it pours — liquid iron!

Ambrosia

Dear Earthlings,

I love it here!
Modad said I have to go to bed at sunset — but didn't say which sunset. Here on HD 188753 Ab there are three suns. It looks cool, but boy, it's hot! I'm outta here.
(P.S. HD 188753 Ab is no oddball — lots of exoplanets in the Milky Way galaxy have more than one sun!)

Ambrosia

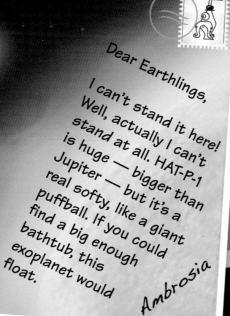

Dear Earthlings,

I can't stand it here!
Well, actually I can't stand at all. HAT-P-1 is huge — bigger than Jupiter — but it's a real softy, like a giant puffball. If you could find a big enough bathtub, this exoplanet would float.

Ambrosia

Dear Earthlings,

Finally, an exoplanet that feels a little more like Earth. OGLE-2005-BLG-390Lb is a rocky planet five times larger than Earth. But since its star is small and doesn't give off much heat, OGLE is cold, only −220°C (−364°F). I think I'll look for somewhere cozier.

Ambrosia

Searching Around Life Stars

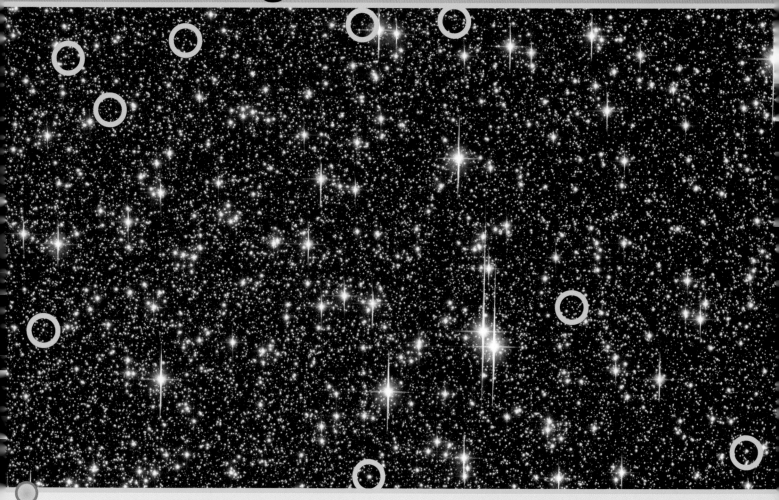

This image from the Hubble Space Telescope shows 150 000 stars. Exoplanets have been found around the stars circled in green. There are many more exoplanets yet to be found in this area of space.

In the race to track down a living exoplanet, the big question is where to look. After all, there are hundreds of billions of stars in the Milky Way galaxy. To narrow down the search, astrobiologists have devised a plan. First, they say, look around "life stars."

Whether a star has what it takes to cook up life depends a lot on its size, and thus how long it shines. The bigger the star, the faster it burns. Some are so big they burn out like cosmic firecrackers in about 3 million years. That's not enough time for life to simmer into existence.

On the opposite end of the size scale are red dwarf stars. They're the smallest and most common stars in the Milky Way galaxy. Although they're not nearly as bright as our sun, they shine for about 200 billion years, plenty of time for life to get started.

One star that we know for sure is the right size for life is our sun, a medium-sized star. It's been burning for about 4.5 billion years. You are living proof that this is long enough for some pretty interesting life to evolve.

So astrobiologists are focusing their search on stars like our sun and red dwarfs, the kind they think might be able to spark life.

The Right Heat

Once you've found a life star, the next step is to check out its "Goldilocks Zone," or habitable zone. This is the area around a star where it's not too hot and not too cold, but just right for there to be liquid water, life's magic ingredient.

Where the Goldilocks Zone is depends on the star's size. If you've ever stood around a campfire you'll know why. The bigger the fire, the farther back you have to go to feel comfortable. It's the same with stars and planets. For a smaller, dimmer star, the Goldilocks Zone would be closer to it than for a bigger, hotter star, such as our sun.

Astrobiologists are looking in the Goldilocks Zone around life stars in search of an exoplanet that's in just the right place for life.

An artist's impression of the giant gas exoplanet HD 189733b, which has water vapour in its atmosphere.

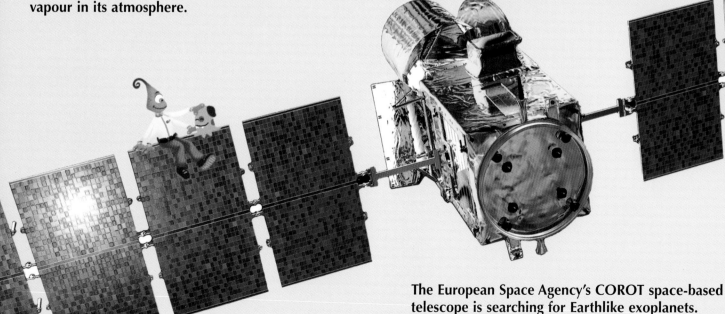

The European Space Agency's COROT space-based telescope is searching for Earthlike exoplanets.

Exoplanets That Rock

Earth is mostly a big chunk of rock and iron, and astrobiologists think an Alien Earth might be, too. Yet most of the exoplanets found so far are giant gas planets. No problem, say astrobiologists. Gas exoplanets indicate that rocky ones can't be far away.

Why? Because of how planets form. A solar system starts out as a huge cosmic cloud of dust and gas. Most of this material goes into making the star. But around the new star swirls a pancake-shaped disk of star-making leftovers. This is the stuff from which planets are born.

The gas closest to a star gets blown far away by the intense heat and winds from the star's surface. So gas planets like Jupiter form far away from their star. Closer to the star, all that's left is sand. Over millions of years the bits of sand crash together to form bigger and bigger rocky pieces and planets, such as our Earth. So rocky planets form nearer to their stars than gas ones.

Astrobiologists think that solar systems all start the same way. So when they discover giant gas planets around a star, they're pretty sure there are smaller rocky ones there, too.

Astrofact

If giant gas planets form far from their star, how do hot Jupiters get so close? Astrobiologists think they form far from their star, then later move closer.

Planets form from orbiting discs of rock and gas around newborn stars.

Where do stars come from? They're made from huge clouds of gas, as seen in this star-forming area called Rho Ophiuchi.

Robert Hurt: Space Artist

How do we get cool images of exoplanets like the one on the next page? Ask Robert Hurt, a space artist. He's an astronomer *and* an artist. His job is to take images collected by NASA's Spitzer Space Telescope and turn them into amazing exoplanet illustrations to help us imagine what alien worlds might actually look like.

Exoplanets are so far away that what the Spitzer telescope sees is often just dots of light. And the telescope takes pictures in black and white. To turn these blurry, black-and-white dots into stellar color images, Robert first talks with the astronomers. He asks them to explain what they've discovered and why it's important. Then he uses his knowledge and imagination to see these alien planets in his mind's eye.

He starts his illustration with a pencil sketch. Next he creates a computer version and adds color. Each color tells part of the scientific story. For example, red indicates hotter regions. Green represents the chemicals associated with life. To create his final "artist's concept," he sometimes uses the same animation software used for TV space shows.

His big dream? To one day see detailed snapshots of exoplanets and compare them with the images he's created.

25

Imagining an Exoplanet

When astronomers using the Spitzer Space Telescope looked at a star named CoKu Tau 4, something was missing. There was a gap in the disk of dust around the young star. Where did the dust go? Astronomers think it might have been swept up by a newborn Jupiter-sized planet.

Space artist Robert Hurt used what astronomers discovered to create this picture of the baby exoplanet.

- The heat from planet formation leaves newborn planets red hot. They glow red like a hot piece of iron.

- The rings are planet-making left-overs. A moon might form from these bands of dust and ice.

- A huge ring of dust and gas still circles the young star. Distant stars are visible above and below the dust ring.

- The dark bands in the exoplanet's atmosphere are cooler areas. They make the newborn giant gas planet resemble a similar planet closer to home — Jupiter.

Space artist and astronomer Robert Hurt created this image of a planet and a nearby star surrounded by planet-forming dust.

A Recipe for Life

One reason astrobiologists think there could be lots of Alien Earths is that the universe is full of the ingredients for life.

The main building block of all life we know is the carbon atom. After water, carbon is the main ingredient from which you're made. It is the backbone of all your body's sugars, fats and proteins. And here's the shocker — every one of your carbon atoms was produced by a star. Yes, you are stardust, and so is every other living thing.

As a star burns, it blasts carbon and other atoms, such as oxygen and iron, into space. These atoms mix in a massive space storm called a molecular cloud. Here individual atoms join to form groups of atoms called molecules. In molecular clouds, scientists have spotted more than 100 different organic molecules, ones made with carbon. These include sugars, alcohols and even juglone, a substance found in walnut shells.

And it is from molecular clouds that stars and planets form — with all the raw materials they need for life to sprout.

NASA's Spitzer and Hubble Space Telescopes teamed up to create this image of a cosmic cloud 1500 light years away called the Orion Nebula. The red and orange wisps in this image are of carbon-rich molecules just like those found in burned toast.

Pass the Meteorite?

Astrobiologists think that when our solar system was formed, most of the organic molecules were far from the sun — well beyond Earth. So how did these raw materials for life get to our planet? Astrobiologists think some of them crash-landed.

The evidence is in meteorites, such as the one that landed with a bang near the small town of Murchison, Australia, in September 1969. Tests revealed that it was formed at the birth of our solar system 4.5 billion years ago, and it is packed with the organic molecules needed for life. Over millions of years meteors may have delivered the ingredients for life to Earth.

Meteorites bombarded the young Earth, perhaps bringing life to the planet.

Astrofact

If you could get your tongue close enough to an old star, you might be surprised. *Hey, it tastes like burned toast!* Stars produce the same black, sooty material that's on a piece of scorched toast — carbon.

Tasty Space Treats

These delicious treats are made of sugars and proteins — much like the molecules in molecular clouds. Warning: this recipe contains peanuts.

250 mL (1 c.)
peanut butter (protein)

250 mL (1 c.)
powdered milk (protein)

300 mL (1 1/4 c.)
icing sugar (sugar)

250 mL (1 c.) honey (sugar)

Shredded coconut
or chopped nuts (optional)

In a medium bowl, combine the first four ingredients. Scoop up the mixture one tablespoon at a time and use your hands to shape it into balls. When you're done, you can roll the balls in shredded coconut or chopped nuts if you wish. Set the balls on a baking tray lined with waxed paper and refrigerate until firm. Makes 24 to 30 out-of-this-world space treats.

First Photo of Alien Earth

Ambrosia checks out the first-ever image of an exoplanet. It's the red dot on the right. The larger background picture is an artist's idea of what the exoplanet and its star might look like. This exoplanet is not a potential Alien Earth because it's a giant gas planet. One day, astronomers hope to take a picture of a small rocky planet that *could* be an Alien Earth.

When astrobiologists finally track down an Alien Earth, the first thing they'll want to do is take a picture of it. Unfortunately, it won't be a pretty image. An Alien Earth will be so far away that the first picture won't be much more than a faint and fuzzy dot of light. But for astrobiologists it will be the most beautiful picture ever taken, because it will be a gold mine of information about the exoplanet.

For starters, the color of the light will give scientists clues about the gases in the planet's atmosphere. And changes in the dot of light over time will reveal much more. For example, if the exoplanet appears to get brighter and then darker on a regular basis, that might indicate the presence of clouds, icecaps, continents or oceans. On Earth, clouds and icecaps are like mirrors, reflecting more than half of the sunlight that hits them. Oceans, on the other hand, look dark because they reflect just a tiny bit of light. If the brightness of the light from an Alien Earth changes at regular intervals, we may be seeing evidence of bright clouds and icecaps and then the much darker oceans.

And the best thing is that light never lies. Light leaving an Alien Earth will carry information unchanged across the Milky Way galaxy, right to an Earthling light detective.

What Will Alien Earth Look Like?

An Alien Earth may not look anything like our planet today but instead resemble Earth in the past. Earth has changed a *lot* since it formed 4.5 billion years ago. Here's a sample of images from Earth's photo album — and what an Alien Earth might look like now.

Water World, **3.9 billion years ago**	**Slimeball Earth,** **2.4 billion years ago**	**Snowball Earth,** **about 750 million years ago**
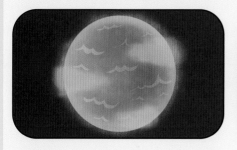		
A single ocean covered almost all of newborn Earth's surface. There was no breathable oxygen in the atmosphere but lots of sulfur, so it smelled like rotten eggs.	Earth's first life was anaerobic — bacteria and blue-green algae that breathed in carbon dioxide, not oxygen. These anaerobic microbes turned the oceans into slimy, oozy, reddish soups.	Geologists (scientists who study rocks) have found evidence of glaciers in the tropics 750 million years ago. At several times in Earth's history our planet might have been covered pole to pole with a thick layer of ice.

Alien Earth in a Computer

Then again, an Alien Earth may not resemble Earth past or present. It may look completely different. Astrobiologists at NASA's Virtual Planetary Laboratory are using computers to create models of possible Alien Earths. They mix information about different kinds of stars, rocky planets and atmospheres to find out which kinds of exoplanets could be alive. These virtual exoplanets guide astrobiologists as they hunt for another living world.

Computer images help us imagine what an Alien Earth might look like.

Long-Distance Life Detector

How will astrobiologists tell whether a distant exoplanet is actually alive? The best place to look for biomarkers, or signs of life, is in a planet's atmosphere. The gases there will provide big hints about whether anyone (or anything) is breathing down below.

To see what's in an exoplanet's atmosphere, astronomers use a technique called spectroscopy. Spectroscopy is the rainbow science because it's based on dividing light into its spectrum, or rainbow, of different colors.

After a rain shower, when the light from our sun passes through droplets of water in the sky, we see a rainbow — sunlight broken into its spectrum of colors, from violet to red.

The light we see coming from an Alien Earth will have passed through its atmosphere. Every chemical in that atmosphere, from water to oxygen, has its own light fingerprint — the pattern of light it absorbs, emits and reflects. So light passing through an exoplanet's atmosphere carries information about the gases there.

Astrobiologists have already used spectroscopy to study the atmospheres of giant gas exoplanets, where they've spotted everything from salt to water. Now they're looking for a rocky exoplanet to study the same way, using spectroscopy to detect gases in the atmosphere that might indicate life.

What gases could be signs that an exoplanet is alive? Two important ones are ozone and water vapor. In Earth's atmosphere ozone gas in the ozone layer protects life from the sun's ultraviolet radiation, and it might do the same on an Alien Earth. And water is key to life as we know it, so it would make a big splash if water vapor (the gaseous form of water) were discovered in an Alien Earth's atmosphere.

The light from a star actually contains all these colors. The dark lines tell us what the star is made of.

An artist's impression of an exoplanet that has an atmosphere, like Earth does.

Red Plants and Little Green Men

But never mind the alien atmosphere. You're probably wondering what alien *creatures* might look like. On that score, astrobiologists say keep a very open mind. Alien life might look so different from life on Earth that at first we might not recognize it.

For example, instead of a world like ours with green plants, we might find an exoplanet with orange, yellow or red trees and grasses. Plants on Earth are green because of how they use sunlight to make sugars, a process called photosynthesis. Our plants get energy from the red and blue parts of sunlight, but reflect the green part. That's what makes plants look green. But on an Alien Earth with a different kind of sunlight and atmosphere, plants might use the green and blue parts of their star's light for energy. If so, the plants would look red. So would good gardeners there have "red thumbs"?

Astrobiologists think that, depending on an exoplanet's star, alien plants might not be green.

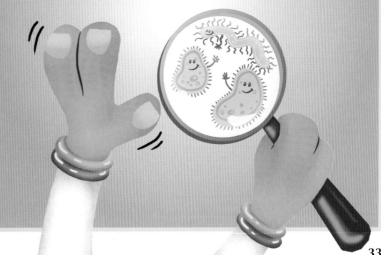

Astrofact

There's a good chance the inhabitants of an Alien Earth will include *very* little "green men" — microbes. For most of the history of life on Earth, about the first 2 billion years, microbes were the only life form. Today there are still more one-celled creatures on Earth than any other kind. The same is probably true on other planets.

Tuning In to Aliens

In our search for an Alien Earth, what we're really hoping to find is not just another living planet but one with *intelligent* aliens — creatures we can communicate with. Then we could talk about everything from alien foods to sports and spaceships.

Astrobiologists looking for intelligent alien life are part of the Search for Extraterrestrial Intelligence (SETI). These scientists are listening for a call from ET using radio telescopes. Just as your radio tunes in to radio waves sent through Earth's atmosphere, a radio telescope picks up radio waves from outer space.

But tuning in to ET isn't as easy as tuning in to your favorite music station. The problem is that the universe is full of naturally produced radio waves, including those from black holes, which are incredibly powerful areas at the centers of galaxies. So SETI scientists tune in to, and record, billions of different frequencies of cosmic radio waves at the same time. Then comes the really hard part: using computers to sift through all these radio waves in search of an alien message.

So far SETI scientists haven't received any calls. But they're not discouraged. They have only listened in on a tiny part of the Milky Way galaxy. They still have high hopes that a cosmic call could come at any time.

An artist's impression of three newly discovered Earthlike exoplanets orbiting their star.

The Allen Telescope Array in California links dozens of antennas together to form one huge, super-sensitive radio telescope. It's so sensitive, it could even eavesdrop on any alien TV signals that leak out into space.

Join the Search for ET

More than five million personal computers are listening for a call from ET, and yours could be, too. Join the search at http://setiathome.berkeley.edu/.

Dan Werthimer: Computers for ET

In the early 1990s, the Search for Extraterrestrial Intelligence (SETI) hit information overload. SETI scientists were tuning in to millions of different cosmic radio channels at once. The problem? They couldn't afford a supercomputer to search all those radio signals for alien messages.

Fortunately, Dan Werthimer had an Earth-sized solution. Dan has always been interested in two things: aliens and computers. As a teenager he programmed some of the first computers to search for SETI signals.

Faced with the information overload, Dan had a brainwave. SETI scientists didn't need one big computer — they could use thousands of small personal computers working together over the Internet.

Dan and other scientists created the SETI@Home program. Through SETI@Home, segments of cosmic radio recordings are sent out to personal computers all around the world. The computers check for possible ET messages and send the results back to SETI@Home. Thanks to Dan, when the first alien radio message arrives, it could be your computer that discovers it!

Earth to Aliens

SETI scientists are not just waiting for aliens to call us — they are creating Earthling greetings to beam into outer space.

But making a "Hello from Earth" message is no easy task. Here on Earth there are hundreds of different languages, and trying to communicate with someone who speaks a different language can feel alien enough. Just imagine trying to make yourself understood to a *real* alien.

Astrobiologists are hoping we can communicate with intelligent aliens by using a universal language — mathematics. They figure that if an alien civilization is able to send and receive radio waves, they must be able to build radios. That means they will have developed technology and science that uses a lot of math.

So while Earthlings and aliens might look and sound very different, mathematically we might *think* the same way, and thus be able to communicate with numbers.

What will an Alien Earth look like? The possibilities are endless.

My Message to ET

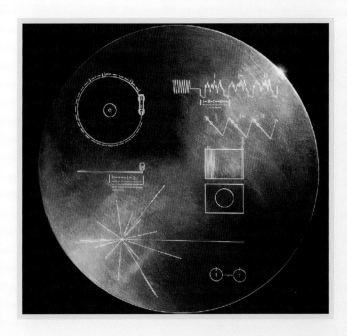

The *Voyager I* and *II* robotic spacecraft launched by NASA in 1977 each carries greetings from Earth on a Golden Record. (A record is a disc used for recording and playing music before CDs and computers took over the job.) Instead of numbers, the Golden Records hold images and sounds that scientists thought best represented Earth and humans. If aliens find these records, they'll hear Earthling music; "Hello!" in fifty-five human languages; calls from many animals, including a whale; and the sound of a mother kissing her baby. What Earth sounds would you put on a CD for aliens?

This message to aliens left Earth in 1977. It has now passed Pluto and is heading for distant stars.

What Are the Odds?

What makes most astrobiologists so optimistic that we'll find aliens to talk with is the Drake Equation. This mathematical tool was developed in 1961 by American astronomer Frank Drake to estimate the number of worlds with intelligent life in the Milky Way galaxy.

Here's how part of the Drake Equation calculates the alien odds:

Number of stars in the Milky Way galaxy = 300 billion
And that's only in our home galaxy, the Milky Way. There are billions more galaxies in the universe.

Number of stars with planets = 150 billion
Astrobiologists think that at least half of the stars in the Milky Way have planets like those in our solar system.

Number of Earthlike planets in the Goldilocks Zone of stars
= 50 billion
About one in every three stars with planets could have rocky, Earthlike planets in the habitable zone where water would be liquid.

Number of planets with
intelligent life = **?**

There's no exact answer to the Drake Equation. But many astrobiologists estimate that right now there could be at least 1000 other intelligent civilizations in the Milky Way galaxy alone.

Earth as Exoplanet

Night after night, as we search the Milky Way galaxy for other planets like ours, aliens might also be searching for us. What would they see?

In the 1960s the *Apollo* astronauts were the first people to take pictures of Earth from outer space. Those images changed the way we think about our planet. For the first time we saw that we really are one world — a big blue marble of life in the blackness of endless space. That view of Earth helped launch the environmental movement. It made us think more about taking care of our planetary home.

Now, thanks to NASA's *Cassini* robotic space-craft, launched in 1997, we are getting new views of Earth, like the one on the right. It shows Earth from far out in our solar system. And, as our knowledge of exoplanets grows, we may come to see ourselves as one living planet among many. Who knows? Maybe your great-great-grandchildren will carry Milky Way passports that say, Planet of birth: Earth.

Cassini's photo of Earth from far out in space reminds us that, to an alien civilization, we *are* Alien Earth — remote, strange and full of mysteries. Imagine what incredible stories wait to be told from other worlds that for now are less than a flicker of light in the night sky.

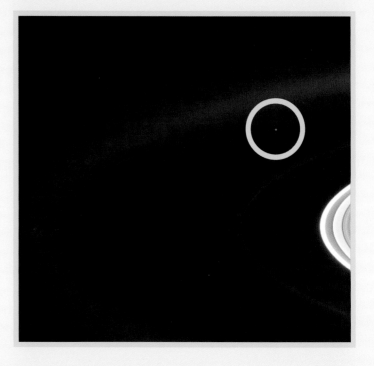

This is a color snapshot of what Earth looks like from 1 500 000 000 km (930 000 000 mi.) away. As NASA's *Cassini* robotic spacecraft passed Saturn, its controllers turned it to take a homeward look. That's the edge of Saturn's rings on the right. And that tiny blue dot (circled in green)? That's us!

Glossary

Alien Earth — a living planet around a star other than our sun

alien life — possible life in the universe other than on Earth

astrobiologist — a scientist who studies life in the universe

astronomer — a scientist who studies the stars and other objects in the universe

atmosphere — the gases that form the outer layer around a planet or star

atoms — the tiny building blocks of all matter. Atoms join together to form molecules.

billion years — a thousand million years (1 000 000 000 years)

exoplanet — a planet outside our solar system

extraterrestrial — beyond the Earth

galaxy — a group of billions of stars, such as our home galaxy, the Milky Way

hot Jupiter — an exoplanet that's mostly gas, like Jupiter, but that's very hot because it's close to its star

microbe — a living organism so small it can't be seen without a microscope

molecule — a group of two or more atoms, such as water (which is made from two hydrogen atoms and one oxygen atom)

moon — a body that orbits a planet. A planet can have many moons.

planet — a large body that orbits a star

robotic spacecraft — an unmanned vehicle sent to explore planets, moons or other objects in space

solar system — a star and the planets, asteroids and meteorites that orbit it

star — a huge ball of hydrogen gas that produces heat and light through nuclear reactions. Stars come in many different sizes and live from several million to 20 billion years.

telescope — a tool for seeing and finding objects in outer space. This includes land- or space-based telescopes (ones that orbit the Earth) and radio telescopes that "see" using radio waves rather than light.

How did we fake the UFO photo on page 7?

We used double-sided tape to tape a coin to the front windshield of a car. Then we sat in the back seat and took a photograph of it.

Photo Credits

Cover: NASA/ESA and G. Bacon (STcI). **pp. 4–5** European Space Agency & NASA, E. Olszewski (University of Arizona). **p. 6** Bottom: NASA. **p. 7** Left: NASA/JPL-Caltech. Right: Apartment 11 Productions. **p. 8** Martin Mach. **p. 9** Top: David J. Baumler. Middle: Michael J. Daly, Uniformed Services University of the Health Sciences, Bethesda, Maryland, USA. Bottom: Woods Hole Oceanographic Institution. **p. 10** Top: NASA and The Hubble Heritage Team (STScI/AURA). Bottom: NASA/JPL-Caltech/Cornell University. **p. 11** Top: NASA/JPL/Malin Space Science Systems. Bottom: NASA. **p. 12** Main image and inset: Expedition Delta of the Mars Society of Canada. **p. 13** Olathe MacIntyre. **p. 14** Top: NASA/JPL. Bottom: NASA. **p. 15** Top: NASA/JPL/Space Science Institute. Bottom: NASA/JPL/University of Arizona. **p. 16** NASA/JPL-Caltech/R.Hurt (SSC). **p. 17** Left: NASA/NSSDC. Right: Dodo, Wikimedia Commons. **p. 18** NASA/JPL. **p. 19** Left and bottom right: Lowell Observatory, J. Hall. Top right: David Charbonneau. **p. 20** Left: David A. Aguilar, Harvard-Smithsonian Center for Astrophysics. Right: NASA, ESA and G. Bacon (STScI). **p. 21** Top: NASA/JPL-Caltech. Middle: David A. Aguilar/Aspen Skies. Bottom: NASA/ESA and G. Bacon (STcI). **p. 22** NASA, ESA, K. Sahu (STScI) and the SWEEPS Science Team. **p. 23** Top: ESA-C. Carreau. Bottom: CNES/D. Ducros. **p. 24** NASA/JPL-Caltech/Harvard-Smithsonian CfA. **p. 25** Top: NASA/JPL-Caltech/C. Lisse (Johns Hopkins University Applied Physics Laboratory). Bottom: Robert Hurt. **pp. 26–27** NASA/JPL-Caltech/R. Hurt (SSC). **p. 28** Credit: NASA/JPL-Caltech/T. Megeath (University of Toledo) & M. Robberto (STScI). **p. 29** David A. Aguilar/Aspen Skies. **p. 30** Main image: ESO PR Photo 14c/05 and inset ESO PR Photo 14a/05 — both: ESO/UCLA/CNRS. Bottom: NASA/JPL-Caltech. **p. 31** NASA/JPL-Caltech. **p. 32** Main image: NASA, ESA, and G. Bacon (STScI). Inset spectrograph: NOAO/AURA/NSF/WIYN. **p. 33** Caltech illustration by Doug Cummings. **p. 34** ESO. **p. 35** Top: Adam Hart-Davis. Right: Dan Werthimer. **p. 36** NASA/JPL-Caltech/R. Hurt (SSC-Caltech). **p. 37** NASA/JPL-Caltech. **p. 38** Top: NASA/JPL/Space Science Institute. Bottom: NASA Goddard Space Flight Center Image by Reto Stöckli (land surface, shallow water, clouds). Enhancements by Robert Simmon (ocean color, compositing, 3D globes, animation). Data and technical support: MODIS Land Group; MODIS Science Data Support Team; MODIS Atmosphere Group; MODIS Ocean Group Additional data: USGS EROS Data Center (topography); USGS Terrestrial Remote Sensing Flagstaff Field Center (Antarctica); Defense Meteorological Satellite Program (city lights).

Index